EMMANUEL JOSEPH

Cultural Catalysts, Mastering the Art of Multinational Leadership and Management

Copyright © 2025 by Emmanuel Joseph

All rights reserved. No part of this publication may be reproduced, stored or transmitted in any form or by any means, electronic, mechanical, photocopying, recording, scanning, or otherwise without written permission from the publisher. It is illegal to copy this book, post it to a website, or distribute it by any other means without permission.

First edition

This book was professionally typeset on Reedsy.
Find out more at reedsy.com

Contents

1. Chapter 1: The Global Leader's Vision — 1
2. Chapter 2: Building Trust Across Borders — 3
3. Chapter 3: The Art of Cross-Cultural Communication — 5
4. Chapter 4: Leading a Diverse Team — 7
5. Chapter 5: Navigating Cultural Conflicts — 9
6. Chapter 6: The Role of Emotional Intelligence — 11
7. Chapter 7: Strategic Thinking in a Global Context — 13
8. Chapter 8: Driving Innovation through Cultural Diversity — 15
9. Chapter 9: Ethical Leadership in a Multinational Setting — 17
10. Chapter 10: The Impact of Technology on Global Leadership — 19
11. Chapter 11: Developing Global Talent — 21
12. Chapter 12: Managing Global Teams — 23
13. Chapter 13: The Role of Corporate Social Responsibility... — 25
14. Chapter 14: Adapting to Change in a Global Environment — 27
15. Chapter 15: The Future of Multinational Leadership — 29

1

Chapter 1: The Global Leader's Vision

In today's interconnected world, global leaders must possess a vision that transcends borders and embraces diversity. They need to understand the nuances of different cultures and how these can be harnessed to drive innovation and growth. The ability to see beyond one's own cultural framework and appreciate the richness of other traditions and ways of thinking is a key attribute of a successful global leader. This chapter explores the key attributes of a global leader and the importance of cultural intelligence in shaping a successful multinational organization.

First and foremost, a global leader must have a clear and compelling vision that inspires and motivates their team. This vision should not only focus on business objectives but also on creating a positive impact on the world. By fostering a multicultural mindset, leaders can create inclusive environments where every voice is valued. Such environments are fertile ground for creativity and innovation, as diverse perspectives lead to more robust problem-solving and decision-making processes.

Understanding and leveraging cultural differences is essential for global leaders. It involves recognizing the unique strengths and contributions of individuals from different cultural backgrounds and creating opportunities for them to thrive. This means being open to different ways of thinking, communicating, and working. By doing so, leaders can build a cohesive and dynamic team that is capable of navigating the complexities of the global business landscape.

Moreover, cultural intelligence is a critical component of effective global leadership. Cultural intelligence, or CQ, refers to the ability to understand, appreciate, and adapt to cultural differences. Leaders with high CQ are better equipped to manage cross-cultural interactions, build strong relationships, and lead diverse teams. Developing cultural intelligence requires ongoing learning and self-reflection, as well as a genuine curiosity and respect for other cultures.

2

Chapter 2: Building Trust Across Borders

Trust is the cornerstone of effective leadership, especially in a multinational context. Building trust across different cultures requires a deep understanding of cultural norms and values. Leaders must be adept at navigating cultural differences and finding common ground to establish strong, trust-based relationships. This chapter delves into the strategies for building trust in a global team, including effective communication, empathy, and transparency.

Effective communication is essential for building trust. Leaders must be clear, consistent, and transparent in their communication. They should also be attentive listeners, showing genuine interest in the perspectives and concerns of their team members. This fosters an environment of mutual respect and understanding, which is crucial for building trust across cultural boundaries.

Empathy plays a significant role in building trust. Leaders who demonstrate empathy can connect with their team members on a deeper level, understanding their emotions, motivations, and challenges. This emotional connection helps to build trust and strengthen relationships. By showing empathy, leaders can create a supportive and inclusive environment where team members feel valued and understood.

Transparency is another key component of trust-building. Leaders should be open and honest about their intentions, decisions, and actions. This helps to build credibility and trust with their team members. Transparency also involves being accountable and taking responsibility for one's actions. When leaders demonstrate transparency, they create a culture of trust and integrity within their organization.

3

Chapter 3: The Art of Cross-Cultural Communication

Effective communication is crucial for any leader, but it becomes even more critical in a multinational setting. Cross-cultural communication involves understanding and respecting cultural differences in language, non-verbal cues, and communication styles. This chapter provides practical tips for improving cross-cultural communication, such as active listening, cultural awareness, and adapting communication techniques to suit different cultural contexts.

Active listening is a fundamental skill for effective communication. It involves fully concentrating, understanding, and responding to what is being said. In a cross-cultural context, active listening helps leaders to understand the unique perspectives and experiences of their team members. By actively listening, leaders can build trust, foster collaboration, and prevent misunderstandings.

Cultural awareness is essential for cross-cultural communication. Leaders must be aware of the cultural norms, values, and communication styles of their team members. This helps them to navigate cultural differences and avoid potential pitfalls. Cultural awareness also involves being open-minded and respectful of different cultural perspectives. By cultivating cultural awareness, leaders can improve their communication and build stronger relationships with their team members.

Adapting communication techniques is crucial for effective cross-cultural communication. Leaders should be flexible in their communication style, adjusting their approach to suit the cultural context. This may involve modifying their language, tone, or non-verbal cues to ensure that their message is understood and well-received. By adapting their communication techniques, leaders can enhance their effectiveness and build stronger connections with their team members.

4

Chapter 4: Leading a Diverse Team

Diversity brings a wealth of perspectives and ideas, but it also presents challenges for leaders. Managing a diverse team requires an inclusive leadership style that fosters collaboration and leverages the strengths of each team member. This chapter discusses the benefits of diversity in the workplace and offers strategies for creating an inclusive environment where everyone feels valued and empowered to contribute.

Inclusive leadership is essential for managing a diverse team. Inclusive leaders create an environment where all team members feel respected, valued, and included. They actively seek out and embrace diverse perspectives, recognizing that diversity leads to better decision-making and innovation. Inclusive leaders also foster a culture of collaboration and open communication, where team members feel comfortable sharing their ideas and opinions.

One of the key benefits of diversity is the range of perspectives it brings. Diverse teams can draw on a wide variety of experiences, knowledge, and skills, leading to more creative and innovative solutions. By leveraging the strengths of each team member, leaders can drive organizational success and stay competitive in a global market.

Creating an inclusive environment requires intentional effort. Leaders should implement policies and practices that promote diversity and inclusion, such as diverse hiring practices, mentorship programs, and inclusive workplace training. They should also lead by example, demonstrating inclusive behaviors and addressing any biases or discrimination within the team. By creating an inclusive environment, leaders can unlock the full potential of their diverse team and achieve greater success.

5

Chapter 5: Navigating Cultural Conflicts

Cultural conflicts are inevitable in a multinational organization, but they can be managed effectively with the right approach. Leaders must be skilled at identifying the root causes of conflicts and addressing them in a constructive manner. This chapter explores common sources of cultural conflicts and provides practical techniques for resolving them, such as mediation, negotiation, and fostering mutual understanding.

Identifying the root causes of cultural conflicts is the first step in resolving them. Leaders should seek to understand the underlying cultural differences and how they may be contributing to the conflict. This requires active listening, empathy, and cultural awareness. By understanding the root causes, leaders can address the conflict more effectively and prevent it from escalating.

Mediation is a valuable tool for resolving cultural conflicts. It involves facilitating a dialogue between the conflicting parties to help them understand each other's perspectives and find a mutually acceptable solution. Mediators should be neutral and impartial, creating a safe and respectful environment for open communication. Mediation can help to resolve conflicts and build stronger relationships within the team.

Negotiation is another effective technique for resolving cultural conflicts. Leaders should use negotiation to find common ground and reach a compromise that satisfies both parties. This requires effective communication, empathy, and problem-solving skills. By negotiating in good faith, leaders can resolve conflicts and maintain a positive and productive team environment.

Fostering mutual understanding is crucial for resolving cultural conflicts. Leaders should encourage team members to learn about each other's cultures and perspectives. This can be achieved through cultural exchange programs, team-building activities, and open discussions about cultural differences. By fostering mutual understanding, leaders can create a more harmonious and collaborative team environment.

6

Chapter 6: The Role of Emotional Intelligence

Emotional intelligence (EI) is a critical skill for leaders in a multinational context. It involves the ability to understand and manage one's own emotions and those of others. Leaders with high EI can navigate the complexities of cross-cultural interactions and build strong, cohesive teams. This chapter examines the components of emotional intelligence and offers tips for developing EI in a global leadership role.

Self-awareness is the foundation of emotional intelligence. It involves recognizing and understanding one's own emotions, strengths, and weaknesses. Self-aware leaders can regulate their emotions and respond appropriately to different situations. By being in tune with their own feelings, they can lead with authenticity and build trust with their team members.

Self-regulation is another important aspect of emotional intelligence. It involves managing one's emotions and impulses, particularly in challenging situations. Leaders who can control their emotional responses are better equipped to handle stress, resolve conflicts, and make rational decisions. Self-regulation also involves being adaptable and flexible, which is essential for navigating the complexities of a multinational environment.

Empathy is a key component of emotional intelligence. It involves understanding and sharing the feelings of others. Empathetic leaders can connect with their team members on a deeper level, fostering strong relationships and creating a supportive and inclusive environment. Empathy also helps leaders to navigate cultural differences and build trust across borders.

Social skills are crucial for leaders with high emotional intelligence. They involve effective communication, conflict resolution, and relationship-building. Leaders with strong social skills can inspire and motivate their team members, create a positive team culture, and navigate the complexities of cross-cultural interactions. By developing their social skills, leaders can enhance their effectiveness and create a cohesive and high-performing team.

7

Chapter 7: Strategic Thinking in a Global Context

Strategic thinking is essential for leaders to guide their organizations towards long-term success. In a multinational context, strategic thinking involves understanding global trends, market dynamics, and cultural factors that impact business decisions. This chapter discusses the importance of strategic thinking and provides a framework for developing and implementing effective strategies in a global environment.

Global awareness is a critical aspect of strategic thinking. Leaders must stay informed about global trends, economic developments, and geopolitical factors that impact their industry. By understanding the broader context, leaders can anticipate changes and adapt their strategies accordingly. Global awareness also involves recognizing the cultural factors that influence consumer behavior and market dynamics.

Market analysis is another important component of strategic thinking. Leaders must conduct thorough market research to identify opportunities and threats in different regions. This involves analyzing market trends, competitor strategies, and consumer preferences. By gaining insights into the market, leaders can develop targeted strategies that address the unique needs and preferences of different cultural groups.

Scenario planning is a valuable tool for strategic thinking. It involves creating different scenarios based on potential future developments and assessing their impact on the organization. This helps leaders to prepare for uncertainties and make informed decisions. Scenario planning also enables leaders to identify potential risks and develop contingency plans to mitigate them.

Implementing effective strategies requires a clear vision and strong execution. Leaders must communicate their strategic vision to their team and align their efforts towards achieving common goals. This involves setting clear objectives, allocating resources, and monitoring progress. By staying focused and adaptable, leaders can navigate the complexities of the global business landscape and achieve long-term success.

8

Chapter 8: Driving Innovation through Cultural Diversity

Cultural diversity can be a powerful driver of innovation. By bringing together individuals with different perspectives and experiences, leaders can foster a culture of creativity and continuous improvement. This chapter explores how to harness the innovative potential of a diverse team and create an environment where new ideas can flourish.

Encouraging diverse perspectives is key to driving innovation. Leaders should create opportunities for team members to share their ideas and opinions. This involves fostering an open and inclusive culture where everyone feels comfortable contributing. By valuing diverse perspectives, leaders can generate a wide range of ideas and solutions.

Collaboration is essential for innovation. Leaders should promote teamwork and collaboration across different cultural groups. This involves creating opportunities for cross-functional and cross-cultural collaboration, such as project teams and brainstorming sessions. By working together, team members can combine their unique strengths and insights to develop innovative solutions.

Providing resources and support is crucial for fostering innovation. Leaders should invest in training, tools, and technologies that enable their team to innovate. This includes providing access to knowledge and information, as well as creating a supportive environment that encourages experimentation and risk-taking. By providing the necessary resources and support, leaders can empower their team to innovate and drive continuous improvement.

Recognizing and rewarding innovation is important for sustaining a culture of creativity. Leaders should acknowledge and celebrate the contributions of their team members. This involves recognizing innovative ideas, providing feedback, and rewarding successful innovations. By creating a culture of recognition and reward, leaders can motivate their team to continue innovating and pushing the boundaries.

9

Chapter 9: Ethical Leadership in a Multinational Setting

Ethical leadership is crucial for maintaining trust and integrity in a multinational organization. Leaders must navigate complex ethical dilemmas and ensure that their actions align with the values and expectations of different cultures. This chapter examines the principles of ethical leadership and provides guidance on making ethical decisions in a global context.

Integrity is the foundation of ethical leadership. Leaders must demonstrate honesty, transparency, and accountability in their actions. This involves being true to one's values and principles, even in challenging situations. By leading with integrity, leaders can build trust and credibility with their team members and stakeholders.

Respect for cultural differences is essential for ethical leadership. Leaders must recognize and appreciate the diverse values and norms of different cultures. This involves being open-minded and respectful of different perspectives, and avoiding actions that may be perceived as disrespectful or insensitive. By respecting cultural differences, leaders can build stronger relationships and navigate ethical dilemmas more effectively.

Fairness is a key principle of ethical leadership. Leaders must ensure that their actions are fair and just, and that they do not favor one group over another. This involves treating everyone with respect and dignity, and making decisions that are in the best interest of the organization as a whole. By promoting fairness, leaders can create an inclusive and equitable environment.

Social responsibility is an important aspect of ethical leadership. Leaders must consider the impact of their actions on society and the environment. This involves making decisions that contribute to the well-being of the communities they operate in, and addressing global challenges such as environmental sustainability and social inequality. By demonstrating social responsibility, leaders can build a positive reputation and create long-term value for their organization.

10

Chapter 10: The Impact of Technology on Global Leadership

Technology has transformed the way leaders manage multinational organizations. From virtual communication tools to data analytics, technology enables leaders to connect with their teams and make informed decisions. This chapter explores the impact of technology on global leadership and offers insights on leveraging technology to enhance leadership effectiveness.

Virtual communication tools have revolutionized the way leaders connect with their teams. Tools such as video conferencing, instant messaging, and collaboration platforms enable leaders to communicate with their team members in real-time, regardless of their location. This enhances collaboration and allows leaders to stay connected with their team, even in a global setting.

Data analytics is another powerful tool for global leaders. By analyzing data, leaders can gain insights into market trends, customer behavior, and operational performance. This enables them to make informed decisions and develop targeted strategies. Data analytics also allows leaders to monitor progress and identify areas for improvement, enhancing their ability to drive organizational success.

Automation is transforming the way leaders manage their operations. By automating routine tasks, leaders can free up time for more strategic activities. This enhances efficiency and productivity, allowing leaders to focus on innovation and growth. Automation also enables leaders to respond more quickly to changes in the market, enhancing their agility and adaptability.

Cybersecurity is a critical concern for global leaders. As organizations become more connected, the risk of cyber threats increases. Leaders must ensure that their organization's data and systems are secure, and that they have robust measures in place to protect against cyberattacks. This involves investing in cybersecurity technologies, implementing best practices, and staying informed about emerging threats.

11

Chapter 11: Developing Global Talent

Attracting and retaining global talent is a key challenge for multinational organizations. Leaders must create an environment that supports the development and growth of their employees. This chapter discusses strategies for developing global talent, including mentorship, training programs, and creating career pathways that align with the aspirations of a diverse workforce.

Mentorship is a powerful tool for developing global talent. Experienced leaders can provide guidance, support, and valuable insights to their mentees, helping them to navigate their career paths and achieve their goals. Mentorship programs can also foster a culture of learning and collaboration, where employees feel supported and encouraged to grow.

Training programs are essential for building the skills and competencies of global talent. Leaders should invest in comprehensive training programs that address the specific needs of their diverse workforce. This may include technical skills, soft skills, and cross-cultural competencies. By providing ongoing learning opportunities, leaders can ensure that their employees are equipped to succeed in a global environment.

Creating career pathways is important for retaining global talent. Leaders should provide clear and transparent career progression opportunities that align with the aspirations of their employees. This involves setting clear expectations, providing regular feedback, and recognizing and rewarding achievements. By creating career pathways, leaders can motivate their employees and foster a sense of purpose and direction.

Fostering a culture of diversity and inclusion is crucial for developing global talent. Leaders should create an environment where all employees feel valued and respected, regardless of their cultural background. This involves implementing policies and practices that promote diversity and inclusion, such as diverse hiring practices, inclusive workplace training, and creating a supportive and inclusive work environment.

12

Chapter 12: Managing Global Teams

Managing global teams requires a unique set of skills, including cultural sensitivity, effective communication, and the ability to motivate and inspire individuals from diverse backgrounds. This chapter provides practical tips for managing global teams, such as setting clear expectations, fostering collaboration, and leveraging the strengths of each team member.

Cultural sensitivity is essential for managing global teams. Leaders must be aware of and respect the cultural differences within their team. This involves understanding cultural norms, values, and communication styles, and adapting their leadership approach accordingly. By demonstrating cultural sensitivity, leaders can build trust and foster a positive team culture.

Effective communication is crucial for managing global teams. Leaders should ensure that their communication is clear, consistent, and transparent. This involves using appropriate communication channels, such as video conferencing, instant messaging, and collaboration platforms, to stay connected with their team members. Effective communication also involves active listening and providing regular feedback.

Fostering collaboration is important for managing global teams. Leaders should create opportunities for team members to work together and share their ideas and perspectives. This may involve organizing team-building activities, cross-functional projects, and virtual collaboration sessions. By fostering collaboration, leaders can create a sense of unity and teamwork within their global team.

Leveraging the strengths of each team member is crucial for managing global teams. Leaders should recognize and value the unique skills and contributions of their team members. This involves assigning roles and responsibilities that align with their strengths and providing opportunities for professional growth and development. By leveraging the strengths of each team member, leaders can enhance the performance and productivity of their global team.

13

Chapter 13: The Role of Corporate Social Responsibility (CSR)

Corporate social responsibility is increasingly important for multinational organizations. Leaders must ensure that their organizations contribute positively to the communities they operate in and address global challenges such as environmental sustainability and social inequality. This chapter explores the role of CSR in global leadership and provides examples of successful CSR initiatives.

Environmental sustainability is a key focus of CSR. Leaders should implement sustainable practices within their organization, such as reducing carbon emissions, minimizing waste, and conserving natural resources. This involves adopting green technologies, promoting energy efficiency, and supporting environmental initiatives. By prioritizing environmental sustainability, leaders can contribute to a healthier planet and enhance their organization's reputation.

Social responsibility is another important aspect of CSR. Leaders should address social challenges such as poverty, education, and healthcare within the communities they operate in. This may involve supporting local charities, providing educational opportunities, and promoting health and wellness programs. By demonstrating social responsibility, leaders can create a positive impact on society and build stronger relationships with their stakeholders.

Ethical business practices are crucial for CSR. Leaders should ensure that their organization operates with integrity and transparency. This involves adhering to ethical standards, promoting fair trade, and preventing corruption. Ethical business practices also involve treating employees fairly and providing a safe and inclusive work environment. By promoting ethical business practices, leaders can build trust and credibility with their stakeholders.

Community engagement is an important aspect of CSR. Leaders should actively engage with the communities they operate in, listening to their needs and concerns, and collaborating on initiatives that address their challenges. This involves building partnerships with local organizations, supporting community development projects, and involving employees in volunteer activities. By engaging with the community, leaders can create a positive social impact and strengthen their organization's connection to the community.

14

Chapter 14: Adapting to Change in a Global Environment

Change is a constant in the global business landscape, and leaders must be agile and adaptable to navigate it successfully. This chapter discusses the importance of change management and offers strategies for leading change in a multinational context, such as fostering a culture of continuous learning and resilience.

Agility is crucial for adapting to change in a global environment. Leaders must be flexible and open to new ideas and approaches. This involves staying informed about global trends and developments, and being willing to adapt strategies and processes accordingly. By demonstrating agility, leaders can respond quickly to changes and seize new opportunities.

Fostering a culture of continuous learning is important for navigating change. Leaders should create an environment where employees are encouraged to learn, grow, and develop new skills. This involves providing ongoing training and development opportunities, promoting a growth mindset, and encouraging innovation. By fostering a culture of continuous learning, leaders can equip their team to adapt to change and stay competitive in a global market.

Resilience is another key attribute for leading change. Leaders must be able to navigate challenges and setbacks, and support their team in doing the same. This involves building a resilient organizational culture, promoting mental and emotional well-being, and providing resources and support for employees. By fostering resilience, leaders can help their team to overcome obstacles and thrive in a changing environment.

Effective change management involves clear communication and strong leadership. Leaders should communicate the vision and objectives of change clearly and consistently, and involve employees in the change process. This involves providing regular updates, addressing concerns, and recognizing and celebrating progress. By leading change effectively, leaders can create a positive and supportive environment that enables their team to embrace change and succeed.

15

Chapter 15: The Future of Multinational Leadership

The future of multinational leadership will be shaped by ongoing global trends, such as technological advancements, demographic shifts, and evolving cultural dynamics. This chapter looks ahead to the future of multinational leadership and provides insights on how leaders can prepare for the challenges and opportunities that lie ahead.

Technological advancements will continue to transform the way leaders manage multinational organizations. Emerging technologies such as artificial intelligence, blockchain, and the Internet of Things will create new opportunities for innovation and efficiency. Leaders must stay informed about these technologies and be willing to adopt and integrate them into their operations.

Demographic shifts will also impact multinational leadership. The global workforce is becoming increasingly diverse, with different generations, cultures, and backgrounds represented. Leaders must be able to navigate and leverage this diversity, creating inclusive environments where all employees feel valued and respected. This involves promoting diversity and inclusion, and creating opportunities for cross-cultural collaboration.

Evolving cultural dynamics will continue to shape the global business landscape. Cultural differences will remain a key consideration for multinational leaders, who must be able to navigate these differences and build strong relationships across cultures. This involves developing cultural intelligence, fostering mutual understanding, and creating inclusive environments.

Sustainability will be an important focus for the future of multinational leadership. Leaders must address global challenges such as climate change, resource scarcity, and social inequality. This involves implementing sustainable practices, promoting ethical business practices, and engaging with communities to create a positive impact. By prioritizing sustainability, leaders can create long-term value for their organization and contribute to a better world.

In conclusion, the future of multinational leadership will be shaped by ongoing global trends and evolving cultural dynamics. Leaders must be agile, adaptable, and culturally intelligent to navigate these changes and seize new opportunities. By fostering a culture of diversity and inclusion, promoting sustainability, and leveraging technology, leaders can create a positive and successful future for their organization.

Cultural Catalysts: Mastering the Art of Multinational Leadership and Management"

In an era where globalization is the norm, leaders must master the art of navigating diverse cultures to drive innovation, foster collaboration, and achieve organizational success. **"Cultural Catalysts: Mastering the Art of Multinational Leadership and Management"** is an essential guide for leaders aspiring to excel in a global environment.

This comprehensive book delves into the critical skills and strategies required to lead effectively across cultures. From building trust and enhancing cross-cultural communication to leveraging the strengths of a diverse team and fostering innovation through cultural diversity, each chapter provides valuable insights and practical tips.

The book covers a wide range of topics, including the importance of emotional intelligence, strategic thinking, and ethical leadership in a multinational setting. It also explores the impact of technology on global leadership, the role of corporate social responsibility, and the challenges of managing global teams.

With real-world examples and actionable advice, "Cultural Catalysts" equips leaders with the tools they need to create inclusive environments, drive organizational success, and make a positive impact on the world. Whether you're an experienced leader or an aspiring one, this book will inspire and empower you to become a catalyst for change in the global business landscape.

www.ingramcontent.com/pod-product-compliance
Lightning Source LLC
LaVergne TN
LVHW020501080526
838202LV00057B/6094